WITHDRAWN

Dry fly

Gnat

Wet fly

Fly imitation

Streamer fly

Chumfeeder

THE YOUNG
FISHING
ENTHUSIAST

JOHN BAILEY

Playing a fish

Bluegill

Soft frog lure

Starting out

Spinner

Plug

A DK Publishing Book

www.dk.com

A DK Publishing Book

www.dk.com

Senior Editor Fiona Robertson **Senior Art Editor** Rebecca Johns

Managing Editor Mary Ling

US Editors Irene Pavitt, Constance Robinson

Managing Art Editor Rachael Foster

Photography Steve Gorton

DTP Designer Almudena Díaz **Production** Kate Oliver

Picture Research Jamie Robinson

The young fishing enthusiasts
Carlene Davis, Harry Devenish, Joanne Gittins, Kristofer Learoyd

First American Edition, 1999
2 4 6 8 10 9 7 5 3

Published in the United States by
DK Publishing, Inc.
95 Madison Avenue
New York, New York 10016

Copyright © 1999 Dorling Kindersley Limited

All rights reserved under International and Pan-American Copyright Conventions. No part of this publication may be reproduced, stored in a retrieval system, or transmitted in any form or by any means, electronic, mechanical, photocopying, recording, or otherwise, without the prior written permisson of the copyright owner.
Published in Great Britain by Dorling Kindersley Limited.

Bailey, John 1951–
     The young fishing enthusiast / by John Bailey.--1st American ed.
        p.   cm.
     Includes index.
     Summary: An introduction to the basic techniques of fishing,
     including advice on tackle, bait, and clothing.
     ISBN 0-7894-3965-4
     1. Fishing--Juvenile literature. [1. Fishing.] I. Title.
SH445.B38 1999
799.1--dc21   99-10042
                                                                          CIP

Color reproduction by Colourscan, Singapore
Printed and bound in Italy by L.E.G.O.

Contents

"The taimen is one of the rarest freshwater fish in the world."

To all young fishing enthusiasts

"**C**ONGRATULATIONS! YOU HAVE DECIDED to take up fishing, in my mind absolutely the best sport in the world. You will find that it takes you to fascinating waters of great beauty, that you catch spectacular fish, learn new skills, and make new friends. Above all, you will experience wild excitement. Perhaps it will be when the first bobber goes under, or when a trout rises to take your fly. Then the reel will shriek, the rod will buckle in your hands, your heart will beat like a drum, and you will know exactly why you've become a fishing enthusiast. Best of luck and tight lines every day you fish."

John Bailey

"This fish was caught in a very remote river in Mongolia. It took me several trips to track the species down."

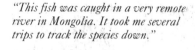

"This golden mahseer has big scales and huge fins."

"Mahseer are the hardest-fighting freshwater fish in the world. They inhabit the quick, clean rivers of India and attract fishing enthusiasts from all over the globe."

"Here I am returning a really super pike to the waters of the Baltic Sea. Big fish in clear water offer great excitement!"

"I am kneeling to land a beautiful Arctic char that has just come up from the sea into one of the rivers in Greenland. Even though I am north of the Arctic Circle, it is still warm enough to do a bit of sunbathing."

"One of my favorite rods – one that I have had for 20 years!"

"Although I love to travel to different countries, I still have time for the ponds and pools where I learned my fishing back in my childhood. Here I am hoping for a carp or a pike."

History of fishing

FOR AS LONG as people have been on Earth, they have wanted to go fishing. In very early times, fishing was just another way of catching food. However, for at least 3,000 years, fishing has also been a sport. The Egyptians and the Romans fished for fun, as have countless men, women, and children ever since. Tackle has improved enormously since those early days, and with the development of space-age materials, it seems likely to continue changing.

Roman pursuits

This engraving dates from the 3rd century BC and supports the theory that the Romans enjoyed fishing. For the more wealthy Romans, fishing was definitely a sport, and one that they could pursue in all the far-flung corners of their empire. Rods were made of either wood or bone, but the hooks were not dissimilar to those used today.

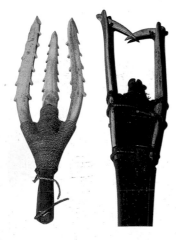

Spears

Spears have been used to catch fish for many hundreds of years and are in fact still used, particularly in the waters of the South Seas. There is a real art to this way of fishing, since you have to take refraction into account. This is the way that the surface reflection distorts the position in which the fish is lying.

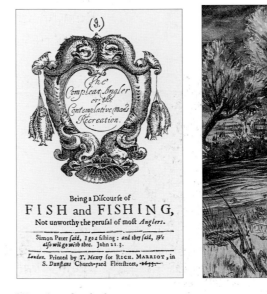

Words of wisdom

The Compleat Angler, published in 1653, is one of the most famous fishing books ever written. It has been published in more than 300 editions and offers advice that can still be followed. The author, Izaak Walton, introduced the idea of fishing purely for enjoyment and for experiencing the pleasure of being close to nature.

An umbrella keeps off the worst of the weather.

Fishing competitions

Competition fishing is very popular all over the world. National and even international matches attract thousands of participants who compete for big prize money. The tackle that is used tends to be very light, so that hundreds of small fish can be landed within the time limits.

Great attention is paid to using bait of the highest quality.

What is a fish?

FISH ARE WONDERFUL, delicate creatures. Their abilities to see, hear, touch, and even smell are very well developed. Remember this when you approach the water's edge. For example, they can see the shadow cast by your body, they can hear and feel your footsteps, and they can even smell sunscreen that has gotten onto the bait from your hands.

The world of fish
There are more than 20,000 known types of fish – more than all mammals, birds, reptiles, and amphibians put together! They come in a variety of shapes and sizes, but all are uniquely adapted to their own environment.

Dorsal fin

The lateral line of a fish runs along the center of the body from the head to the tail. On this mirror carp, it is lined with big scales.

Eye

Nostrils

Mouth

Lips

The gill flap, called the operculum, is a hard, bony area designed to give the fish maximum protection.

The pectoral fins are usually large to help produce bursts of speed.

A layer of slimy mucus protects against disease.

Pelvic fin

The anal fin, situated down the body toward the tail, helps stabilize the fish in a current.

Anatomy of a fish
The body of a fish is tightly packed with sensitive organs, such as the heart, liver, swim-bladder, and stomach. Remember this when you hold a fish: if you squeeze it too tightly, these organs will be crushed, the fish will feel pain, and it could even die.

The kidney is situated centrally, close to the backbone.

The brain coordinates all the fish's actions.

The eye may be large, especially in night feeders.

The delicate gills allow the fish to absorb oxygen from the water.

Eggs are produced in the ovary.

Nutrients are absorbed into the blood via the intestines.

The heart pumps blood to the gills and around the body.

Swimming
Fish propel themselves through the water by pushing against it. Some do this by wriggling in a series of sideways curves; others move their tail area from side to side. This sequence shows the S-shaped wave that passes along the body of a dogfish as it swims.

Note how the S-shaped wave that propels the fish through the water is beginning to appear.

Pectoral fin

Pelvic fin

The dogfish swings its head to the right slightly to start the swimming movement.

The "peak" of the wave is now in the upper region of the fish between the pectoral and pelvic fins.

Living habits

Some fish live solitary lives, but most, especially small fish, live in large groups called schools. Schools are useful for defense. Big predators become confused when they see large numbers of fish break up and flee in panic. Schools of fish develop strong social instincts, and if the water is clear, you can even recognize leader fish, which dictate every movement.

Fish often like physical contact and will rub their bodies together.

Spawning brown trout lay their eggs in a hollow in the gravel.

Fish spawning

All fish spawn, or reproduce, in order to keep their populations alive. Different fish spawn at different times of the year. Salmon and trout spawn in the winter, whereas carp and most other bottom-feeding fish spawn as the water begins to warm up in the spring.

Life cycle

The transition from egg to fully grown fish is a very perilous one, and only a fraction of the eggs laid even get as far as hatching. This sequence shows the development of a young rainbow trout.

Blood vessels have already developed.

Eyes are clearly visible.

The fish is emerging.

1 After the egg is laid, the fish's body starts to take shape within the transparent egg and its outline is clearly visible.

2 The young trout is nearly ready to hatch and can be seen moving around in the egg.

3 The fish has broken through the soft case of the egg and is preparing to wriggle out.

The young fish has plenty of food in its yolk sac when it hatches.

This rainbow-colored band gives the rainbow trout its name.

At this stage, the young trout is called a fry.

4 The young trout has now hatched and is called an alevin. The yolk sac will gradually disappear.

5 Black stripes on the young trout's body have developed, giving it camouflage from predators.

6 The fully developed rainbow trout is a beautiful fish. The female will go on to lay thousands of eggs of her own over her breeding years.

Dorsal fin

Tail

Water will be displaced as the fish powers forward.

The snout of the fish moves to the right again, and another S movement begins.

The wave has now moved farther down the body, and the fish is bending at the dorsal fin.

There is real power being produced now as the muscular movement reaches the hindquarters of the fish and the tail begins to thrust to the right.

This wave's peak finally reaches the tail, and the fish is propelled forward.

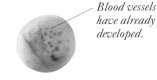

Fish and their food

THERE IS AN OLD SAYING that sounds complicated, but it is quite true: The key to fishing is to put the right bait to the right fish at the right time in the right place in the right way! To get everything correct demands a real knowledge of the fish, and, above all, you have got to know what your chosen quarry wants to eat. We have selected four of the world's most popular fish to show their different diets and ways of feeding.

Carp feed to a great extent by eyesight. Their vision is very good in clouded water and at night.

Carp

Of all fish, the carp probably has the most varied of diets and will eat virtually anything, from weeds to dead fish. Although the mouth of the carp is toothless, the throat-teeth are incredibly strong and can crush the shells of mussels or crayfish.

Perch

The perch is a typical predator that likes to feed only on living organisms. When small, perch feed on worms and insects, but as soon as they reach 8 in (20 cm) or more in length, they move over to an almost exclusively fish diet. They also eat their own young.

The dorsal fin is held erect when hunting.

The distinctive stripes give the perch effective camouflage when mounting an ambush.

The tail fin is relatively small, so the perch relies on its body muscles for power.

The mouth is hinged, allowing it to open very wide to swallow large prey.

The sharp gill flap offers some protection against predators.

The stomach can hold prey one-third of its body weight.

The scales tend to be quite rough to the touch, especially just before spawning.

Sturgeon

The sturgeon is primarily a fish eater, but it can also uproot and devour creatures living in the bottom mud and slime. It uses its long, sharp nose to probe in the silt, looking for food. Its mouth can telescope open like a huge funnel and vacuum up food. A 10-lb (4.5-kg) carp or pike offers no problem to these fish, which can weigh over 300 lb (136 kg).

The sturgeon's eyes are small, so it relies more on touch and smell when hunting.

Most species have a bony ridge along the back. The armored plates are called scutes.

The sturgeon uses its long whiskers to feel for food.

The mouth appears small, but it can telescope out to vacuum up food.

A bony lateral line runs along the length of the body.

The dorsal fin is raised when the carp swims quickly or is hungry. It is lowered when it rests.

These big scales give the fish some protection. They can be used to tell how long the fish has lived.

Mirror carp are recognized by their unique scale clusters, which are very much like our own fingerprints.

Carp are often deep-bodied. Big fish have huge appetites and can consume large amounts of food.

This huge tail fin gives the carp its amazing power.

Sunfish

Sunfish, or sunnies, like water containing weeds, which is full of their favorite foods. The fish hunt for the larvae of insects, fish fry, small mollusks, and earthworms. Mayfly and stonefly larvae are also favorites, and sunfish will even take adult flies that have fallen into the water.

The dorsal fin is held erect during feeding.

The tail is rounded in profile and fairly small.

The mouth can open wide to snatch large insects.

A large eye helps the fish to home in on its prey.

The body stripes give the fish protection from bigger predators.

Large bottom fins give stability in the water.

The triangular dorsal fin is often seen cutting the surface of the water as the fish hunts.

The bony ridge continues along the top of the tail fin.

Eating habits

Fish have various ways of eating, depending on the shape of their mouth and their diet.

Seizing

The pike seizes its food. It approaches its prey with speed, opens its jaws, and sucks in the food with a rush of water. Then it clamps down hard with needle-sharp teeth.

Snatching

Many species, such as black bass, panfish, and trout, come to the surface to grab a land insect that has just entered their world. They often do this violently, with a splash.

Slurping

Carp slurp down food between extended lips. Bobbing baits are simply drawn down into the vortex the carp creates. Sometimes you will see bubbling and hear sucking sounds.

Sucking

Many fish, especially bottom feeders, suck up bait from the riverbed. They telescope out their lips, which creates a vacuum and allows water and food to be drawn into their mouths.

All geared up

ALL YOU NEED when you start fishing are some basic items. Tackle shops have a wide range of rods, reels, bobbers, leads, spinners, and hooks to choose from. Other essential items include warm clothes, an umbrella to keep off the rain, and a strong tackle box for all your equipment. A fold-up chair may come in handy too! However, try to avoid going to the waterside so loaded down that you cannot stay mobile and search for new swims.

Your gear

Once you have collected your gear, it is a very good idea to lay it all out before you go to the water's edge. This helps you to familiarize yourself with everything and also allows you to check that you have not forgotten anything. Make sure you clean your tackle thoroughly after each trip and store it in a dry place.

Your first rod should be light and comfortable. Make sure you take care of it.

There are lots of different seats on the market. Look for one that is easy to carry and fairly inexpensive. It should also be well made so that it lasts.

A strong tackle box is essential for keeping everything together.

You will need a rod rest if you are going bait fishing.

Slingshot

Line

Reel

Bait box

Sunglasses

If you are thinking of going out in a boat to fish, then a life jacket is an absolute necessity, even if you are a strong swimmer.

Fish will eat almost anything that we eat, including cheese and spicy sausage!

You will need separate fly boxes for your dry and wet flies. Choose strong, sturdy boxes that close properly to prevent moisture from getting in.

Make sure you carry a selection of terminal tackle. This will allow you to present your bait properly in any type of weather or water condition.

Choose a hat with a broad brim when fishing in sunshine. This not only keeps the sun out of your eyes, but also helps you see more easily in bright light.

Although they are not strictly necessary, you will find that most experienced fishing enthusiasts use binoculars to scan the water for any sign of feeding fish.

Safety near water

Always be aware of currents and hidden depths near water. Look for this or a similar symbol to indicate situations where you need to be extra careful.

Chest waders

There is no doubt that chest waders give you a definite advantage by allowing you to get close to the fish and present your bait in any current. Never put yourself in danger by wading into areas you are unsure of.

These waders are made of a special breathable fabric, so you do not get hot when you walk.

Wear a number of thin layers, instead of one thick one.

Most hip waders are made of rubber.

Hip waders

For fishing in shallow waters, hip waders are ideal. Choose a light pair, with a good grip on the soles and lightweight uppers that can be folded down to transform the waders into boots. Again, always be sure you stay in your depth.

Handy gloves

It is important to keep warm while you are fishing; otherwise, it will be difficult to concentrate and you will want to go home. Since your fingers and toes often feel the cold first, thick socks and gloves are a good idea.

This slit is useful for feeling the line.

These gloves are made of a special material called Neoprene, which is very warm and water-resistant.

The thumb and finger pieces fold back.

These fold-back fingertips allow you to tie knots or bait the hook quickly and easily – and still keep warm!

Choose your footwear carefully. Look for a good grip and some waterproofing.

A selection of bobbers to suit all water conditions

A container of split shot is essential, especially if you are bobber fishing.

Tackle box

A tackle box like this one can hold an enormous amount of tackle, providing you pack it carefully! Plan what you are going to put on each of the different levels and try to stick to it. The clear lid lets you see that everything is in its place.

Your rod is a very precious item, so always store it in a protective bag or case after you have used it. Clean it thoroughly after each trip to make it last longer.

Choose a soft mesh for your landing net because this is kinder on the fish. Whenever possible, keep the net in the water as you unhook the fish.

Fishing tackle

THE EQUIPMENT you will need
will vary according to whether you
want to fish mainly in freshwater or
saltwater. Look for reliable tackle that
is fairly inexpensive. It is especially
important to choose the right lines and
hooks, because if they fail you, the
fish will be lost. You will find that most
tackle dealers are happy to spend time
advising you, since they know that a
happy customer will always return.

Flies

There are literally thousands of fly patterns around the
world, but in general you should aim to fish dry flies on
the surface, nymphs toward the bottom, and streamer-type
flies quickly through mid-water.

Dry fly

Mini-lure

Fly imitation

Imitation shrimp

Imitation caddis

Streamer fly

*The feathers move
in the water.*

Bobbers

There are differently shaped bobbers for still and running
water (see pages 28–29), so check carefully that you have
the right bobbers with you for the day's fishing ahead.
If in doubt, choose a heavier bobber, which will always
give you more control over the prevailing conditions.

*An Avon bobber
for rivers*

*The transparent stem of this bobber
makes it almost invisible to the fish.*

An Onion bobber for still water

A loaded waggler for still water

Spinning rod

Most spinning rods
are fairly short so you
can work intriguing
areas under low-lying
trees. The screw
fitting on the reel seat
stops the reel from
working loose during
repeated casting.

Cork handle

Eye whipping

*The reel spool
is filled nearly
to the brim
with line.*

Open-faced fishing reel

The fixed-spool reel is used for all
types of bait fishing. It is very easy
to cast with, and modern varieties
have reliable drags to allow
you to give line to running fish.

Fly rod

The fly rod is a
delicate wand of a tool.
Choose one that feels
comfortable, and you'll
be able to fish all day
without getting tired.

Reel seat

Fly-fishing reel

Compared with an open-faced
reel, a fly-fishing reel tends to be
quite simple and straightforward.
Check that the reel has an
adjustable drag.

*The holes let water
drain from the line.*

*The blade
revolves on
the surface.*

Top-water plug

Surface plug

Plugs

There are many different types of plug,
from those that float on the surface to
those that bounce along the bottom.
Color is also very important – go for
light, even neon colors if the water is
cloudy, or subdued colors if it is clear.
Always take a selection with you.

Shallow diver

*This type of lure
will send lots of
vibrations through
the water.*

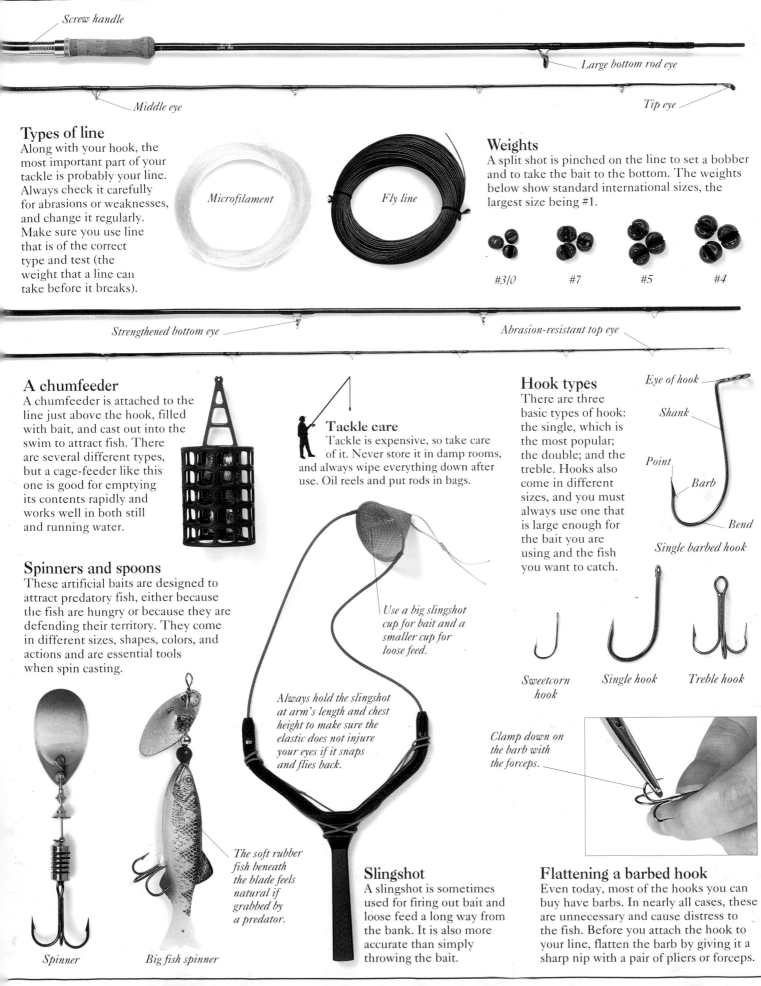

Screw handle

Large bottom rod eye

Middle eye

Tip eye

Types of line

Along with your hook, the most important part of your tackle is probably your line. Always check it carefully for abrasions or weaknesses, and change it regularly. Make sure you use line that is of the correct type and test (the weight that a line can take before it breaks).

Microfilament

Fly line

Weights

A split shot is pinched on the line to set a bobber and to take the bait to the bottom. The weights below show standard international sizes, the largest size being #1.

#3/0   *#7*   *#5*   *#4*

Strengthened bottom eye

Abrasion-resistant top eye

A chumfeeder

A chumfeeder is attached to the line just above the hook, filled with bait, and cast out into the swim to attract fish. There are several different types, but a cage-feeder like this one is good for emptying its contents rapidly and works well in both still and running water.

Tackle care

Tackle is expensive, so take care of it. Never store it in damp rooms, and always wipe everything down after use. Oil reels and put rods in bags.

Hook types

There are three basic types of hook: the single, which is the most popular; the double; and the treble. Hooks also come in different sizes, and you must always use one that is large enough for the bait you are using and the fish you want to catch.

Eye of hook

Shank

Point

Barb

Bend

Single barbed hook

Spinners and spoons

These artificial baits are designed to attract predatory fish, either because the fish are hungry or because they are defending their territory. They come in different sizes, shapes, colors, and actions and are essential tools when spin casting.

Use a big slingshot cup for bait and a smaller cup for loose feed.

Always hold the slingshot at arm's length and chest height to make sure the elastic does not injure your eyes if it snaps and flies back.

Sweetcorn hook   *Single hook*   *Treble hook*

Clamp down on the barb with the forceps.

The soft rubber fish beneath the blade feels natural if grabbed by a predator.

Slingshot

A slingshot is sometimes used for firing out bait and loose feed a long way from the bank. It is also more accurate than simply throwing the bait.

Flattening a barbed hook

Even today, most of the hooks you can buy have barbs. In nearly all cases, these are unnecessary and cause distress to the fish. Before you attach the hook to your line, flatten the barb by giving it a sharp nip with a pair of pliers or forceps.

Spinner   *Big fish spinner*

Getting ready to fish

AT FIRST SIGHT, the amount of fishing tackle that you need can seem pretty daunting. But don't worry. After just a few trips, you'll get used to what everything does and how to assemble it quickly and easily. Concentrate on getting good-quality, basic gear that you are happy with and can trust in every situation; the more advanced items can come later.

1 Make sure that the ends of the pieces to be joined are very clean. Push them together until you feel the fit is absolutely secure.

A light spinning rod like this one is perfect for catching small bass and sunfish.

Attaching a reel

1 Push the lower reel foot firmly into the reel seat, which is situated on the rod butt.

2 Make sure the upper reel foot is safely secured by turning the locking ring.

3 Once the reel is screwed in firmly, hold the line tightly with your index finger.

4 To begin casting, flip the bail arm over.

Putting the rod together

Some rods are just one piece, but most come in two or three lengths that have to be joined together. When you first start fishing, use a 9-ft (3-m) rod.

Lower the rod to help you put the line through the top eyes.

Make sure you keep the eyes clean by wiping them occasionally with a cloth and some soapy water. Replace worn or cracked eyes.

2 Look down the rod to make sure the eyes are all lined up correctly. This is extremely important. If they are not, you will find it difficult to cast.

3 With the bail arm of the reel open, pull the line off the reel and thread it through the eyes. Watch out for tangles around the reel handle.

Grip the hook firmly between the thumb and index finger of your left hand.

4 Once the reel is safely on the rod and the line is through the eyes, shut the reel bail arm (turn reel handle once) and begin to put the tackle and bait on the end of the line.

Make sure the bail arm is open as you thread the line through the eyes.

The ideal location
Now for the really hard part – the moment you turn fishing detective. Both still waters and rivers can look like very large, forbidding places at first. Where do you start? The answer is to avoid rushing in and setting up your gear at the first available place. Spend time walking around the water looking for any signs of fish or for the places you think they might be hiding, such as reeds, islands, and lily pads.

Tying a clinch knot

Everyone who fishes needs to know how to tie a basic, secure knot. There are many different types, which can be bewildering at first. However, it is possible to use just one type of knot for attaching hooks, spinners, and whatever else you will need throughout your fishing career – the clinch knot.

Preventing friction
To prevent a knot from slipping, wet it with water. This will reduce any friction that might occur and will prevent the line from being damaged.

1 Push about 6 in (15 cm) of line through the hook eye. Make a big loop and put the spare end under the main line.

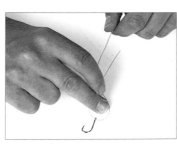

2 Use your right hand to keep the loop open, and with your left hand, move the line counter-clockwise around the loose end.

3 Repeat this counter-clockwise movement about five times. Use your finger to keep the loop open.

Remember to keep your fingers clear of the hook point.

4 Push the end of the spare line through the open loop with your left hand. Hold the loop firmly in your right hand.

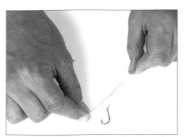

5 Start to tighten the knot, using your left hand to pull the main line and your right hand to pull the spare line.

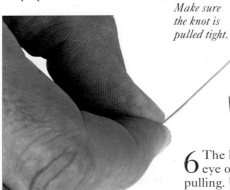

Make sure the knot is pulled tight.

6 The knot forms above the eye of the hook as you keep pulling. Use clippers to trim spare line close to the loop.

Basic casting

WHEN YOU CAST, you simply use your rod and reel to flick the line, tackle, and bait out into the water where the fish will find it. It is one of the most essential skills in fishing, because you won't catch anything on the bank! However, it is important not to be overwhelmed by the techniques involved in casting. Modern tackle has made casting much easier, and you should be able to master it in a few sessions.

Basic technique

Before you begin the casting action, make sure you are standing in a comfortable position. Aim to make the cast a smooth, unhurried motion. The rod, reel, and line should do all the work for you. When you first begin casting, concentrate on accuracy rather than distance. Try to get your bait to land exactly where you want it to. Practice at home with a large metal washer as tackle and a bucket as a target. This will save time at the riverbank.

If your rod is too far back as the casting begins – at nine o'clock for example – you will lose some control.

A peaked cap will shade your eyes from the sun.

Move smoothly so the line does not tangle.

Try to keep the rod as steady as possible.

Stand with your feet apart.

1 Look to where you want to cast. Trap the line against the reel stem with your finger, then move the bail arm over with your left hand.

2 Still with your eyes on the target area, begin to move the rod backward. Slide your left hand down to the butt of the rod.

3 Watch your tackle to be sure it does not tangle as you move the rod over your shoulder. Let your bait hang about 36 in (90 cm) beneath the rod tip.

4 Wait for your tackle to settle as it hangs over your shoulder. Pause to make sure that everything is tangle-free before making the all-important cast.

The correct grip

It is important that you get used to handling the basic equipment as soon as possible. Put the rod and reel together in the tackle shop before you make any purchase. Buy a reel that is the right size for you, or you will find that your fingers have difficulty stretching to the reel's controls and line.

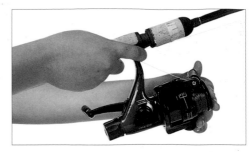

1 Hold the rod in your right hand. The bail arm should be closed.

2 Take the line from the reel and trap it under your index finger. Start to move the bail arm with the other hand.

Bail arm

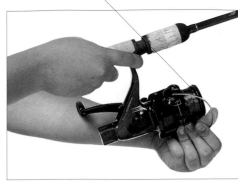

3 Move the bail arm over until it is fully open. You will probably hear a click that will tell you this action is complete.

4 You are now ready to cast. Hold the line tight while the rod is going through the casting arc (see below), and don't let go of the line too early.

5 Once your rod has moved to the one o'clock position, you can let go of the line, allowing it to fly off the reel.

Keep your finger clear of the flying line.

Keep your feet apart and your body balanced throughout the cast.

Not too tight!
Allow the main weight that you are casting to swing about 36 in (90 cm) from the rod tip. Any more or less, and you could get into a terrible tangle.

When the cast is finished, wind the reel handle to close the bail arm, and you are ready to start fishing.

5 Now in one quick, smooth movement, bring the rod over your shoulder to the two o'clock position, lifting your finger to let the line fly out as you do.

6 Finish the cast off with the rod held somewhere between two and three o'clock. Don't go too low or the bait will land with a fish-frightening splash!

The clock face

The positions on the clock face are used to describe the rod movements during casting. At the start of casting (stage 4), your rod should be pointing to ten o'clock. At one o'clock, you will be letting go of the line with your finger. The cast is over when the rod is between two and three o'clock.

Fly fishing

THE MAJOR CONCERN of most beginners when fly fishing is how to cast. Don't worry. All you have to master is the overhead cast, which is the basis of all the other cast forms. You can learn fly casting in a few hours – try practicing at home on the lawn. Remember that presenting the right fly in the right place is much more important than straining to cast at the horizon.

A dry fly floats on the surface to attract a rising fish.

Choosing a fly

Watch the water carefully, and if you see rings, indicating that the fish is rising, try a dry fly. If there is no surface activity, start with a nymph pattern.

Fly rod

Fly rods tend to be light and responsive, and you should be able to handle one all day without getting tired. The reel sits right at the bottom of the rod for better balance.

Fly casting

The overhead cast entails lifting the line off the water and sending it straight out behind you. This is called the back cast, and the weight of the shooting line bends the rod and gives it its power. Once the line is fully extended, you then move the rod forward and the line whistles through the air to place the fly on the water before you. Practice will very soon make perfect.

Wade carefully
Never wade so far out that you put yourself in danger. Remember that even in shallow water, the current can still be very swift and strong.

The ideal location

This picture shows the perfect spot for fly fishing. The water runs quickly over the gravel, then deepens slightly and slows down. Trout and grayling especially love this clean, well-oxygenated water, and their favorite food lives among the stones on the riverbed.

Hold the rod firmly in your casting hand, well above the reel.

Make sure your rod stops at about the ten o'clock position on your back cast.

1 Lift the line off the water and begin the back cast. Try to lift the line in one smooth, continuous motion, keeping your wrist fairly straight. Do not be timid but put plenty of power into the action.

2 It is a good idea to look over your shoulder to see what the line is doing. Let the line straighten out before you begin the forward cast. Don't let your rod fall too low behind you, and keep the line off the bank.

Retrieve the line slowly and carefully in the fingers of your noncasting hand.

Tread carefully
Walk slowly into the river, since the sound of crunching gravel may frighten the fish.

Keep your hand, wrist, and rod in a straight line and hold the rod firmly, so that the rod nestles in your forearm.

Always wear protective glasses when you are fly fishing to shield your eyes from stray flies.

Vary the retrieve to make the fly look as realistic as possible.

3 After completing the forward cast, the line shoots through the rod eyes and places the fly on the water a good way beyond you. To avoid a splashy cast, aim your fly at a spot about 3 ft (1 m) above the surface. Don't let your rod tip drop too close to the water or you will find that the line goes down in a messy heap.

4 As you retrieve your fly, watch out for any sign of a take. Sometimes you will feel a tug, but on other occasions you will simply see your fly line either pause or shoot forward a couple of inches. Strike at once. When the fly is about 16 ft (5 m) away from you, move again into your next back cast.

Flies in action

THE REAL SKILL of fly fishing is knowing exactly what the fish are feeding on in the natural world. You can then attempt to imitate the real insect with an artificial one. To master this skill, you will have to watch the water very carefully and build up a picture of how the fish are behaving at different times of the day. This may sound difficult, but it is a fascinating way to fish.

Watching the water
It is very important to keep a low profile and avoid frightening the fish at all costs. Approach stealthily, and try to get as close to them as possible.

Surface feeding
One of the most exciting sights for anyone who enjoys fly fishing is a trout coming to the surface to take flies. Sometimes it makes a splashy movement; at other times, you will just hear a slurp and see the fish's nose. Try to identify the fly being taken and present one of your own flies to look as close as possible to the real insect.

Artificial mayflies
Compared with other flies, mayflies are very large and, therefore, fairly easy to present to the trout in a convincing way.

Grey Wulff

The real thing
Swarms of adult mayflies are found near rivers throughout the summer. Often called "dayflies" because their lives are so short, mayflies die after mating.

Cut-wing green Drake

Closing in!

There is not a more exciting sight in all of fishing than to watch a trout moving in on your fly – either above or below the surface. Often, a trout will get very close to the fly and even follow it for a while before making a decision. Sometimes it pays to stop retrieving and let the fly sink a little in the water. Other times, it is better to speed up and perhaps lift the fly to the surface, so that the trout thinks it is escaping and makes an instant decision to take it!

Wet flies

Traditional wet flies give the impression of food, rather than actually imitating insects. Wet flies such as the Butcher are tied to attract the trout's attention as they move through quick water.

Butcher

Soldier Palmer

Nymphing for trout

The word "nymphing" actually describes presenting the trout with small flies that represent very common items on their daily menu. These items include the nymphs or larval stages of flies, as well as other small aquatic creatures, such as tiny beetles, snails, and shrimps. Fish them slowly and carefully.

Trout love water shrimp.

This artificial shrimp looks very much like the real thing.

Shrimp

Gammarus water shrimp

Here, my Polaroid glasses give me an excellent view of what is happening in the trout's kingdom.

Freshwater shrimp

Freshwater shrimp cannot survive in polluted water, so their presence is a sure sign that the water is clean. Make sure that your imitation shrimp are weighted well.

Nymphs

Mayfly nymphs live for about a year underwater. They are a favorite food of trout. Imitation nymphs should look like small, dark food items so that they do not arouse suspicion. Move them slowly through the water with small jerks.

Mayfly nymph

Marabou nymph

Lure fishing

LURE FISHING is one of the most exciting ways of catching predatory fish. Pike, perch, bass, trout . . . there is an endless list of fish that will gobble these plastic, metal, or wood creations, mistaking them for real fish. There are three types of lures. Spinners and spoons are usually made of metal and either wobble or spin through the water in the same way as real fish. Plugs are made of wood or plastic and work in a number of ways: along the surface of the water, in mid-water, or deep along the bottom.

The ideal location

When you are lure fishing, it pays to search the water and not stay too long in any one position. A spot like this is ideal – big predators like slack water just off the main current, and some often lie right by the bank.

Always use a wire trace if you think that pike are present, as their sharp teeth cut through monofilament.

Attention to detail

Predatory fish are eagle-eyed, and a good plug should resemble a natural fish very closely. Look for realistic eyes, scale patterns, and a shiny finish.

Make sure that the hooks on your lure are strong enough for the fish you want to catch.

Lure rod

The ideal lure rod is light but with some power to give you control over a big fish. Look for a rod about 9 ft (3 m) long.

Careful approach

Predatory fish are extremely wary, so approach the water carefully or you might scare the fish before you have even started!

Working a lure

Never work your spoon, spinner, or plug in a mechanical, unthinking sort of way. Instead, try to make a big predator think that this strange wood, metal, or plastic creation is in fact a living, breathing, swimming prey fish! Look out for all possible hiding places under fallen trees, among weeds, or along the bank. Cast carefully and accurately, and constantly move the rod tip around to create a change of direction.

1 Make sure that your lure is swinging about 3 ft (1 m) from your rod tip before you begin to cast. It is a good idea to have a quick look at the lure to check that it is fairly still before you begin. Also look closely at where you want the lure to land. Make sure you are standing comfortably and safely, and then begin the cast.

Search out the edge of the current, as well as slack water.

The drag on your reel should be precisely set so that it will give line to a big running fish.

2 Watch the river and the lure as it flies out across the water. As the lure approaches your chosen spot, slow the line with your fingers so that it lands exactly where you want it to. Work the lure close to the surface. Let it stop sometimes, as though it is resting, then quickly jerk it across the water, as though it is in a panic and trying to escape from a predator it has just spotted.

3 Very often, predators will follow a lure right to the bank before deciding to attack. If you move the lure out too quickly, there is every chance you will snatch it from the jaws of the fish. So watch the lure very carefully until it is right at your feet, before lifting it out of the water. Stand a little ways back from the riverbank to avoid being spotted by any approaching predator.

Lures in action

O NE OF THE REAL SKILLS of lure fishing is to know exactly which type of lure – spinner, spoon, or plug – to use in any given situation. To get the most out of this type of fishing, you should keep moving around the river or lake, looking for all kinds of underwater obstructions and water features that will attract fish. Each area will demand a slightly different approach and lure, which is why it is important to build up a collection of lures. You can then experiment with different depths and techniques. Always make your lure look as lifelike as possible.

The ideal location
Search out any areas that might offer a predator good ambush opportunities. Fish such as pike and perch like to wait near reed beds, close to weeds, or beneath overhanging trees, where they are almost invisible to schools of passing prey fish.

Fish awareness
The use of treble hooks on lures can sometimes be dangerous to the fish if they are in an aggressive taking mood. Always try to use a spoon with just a single hook and be sure that the barb has been flattened for easy removal.

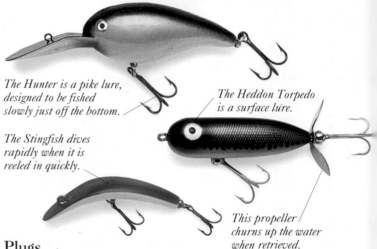

The Hunter is a pike lure, designed to be fished slowly just off the bottom.

The Heddon Torpedo is a surface lure.

The Stingfish dives rapidly when it is reeled in quickly.

This propeller churns up the water when retrieved.

Plugs
A plug is designed to look and move in the same way as a small prey fish, which often swims in distress. Plugs can be used for any depth of water. Work them slowly in areas that might contain big predators.

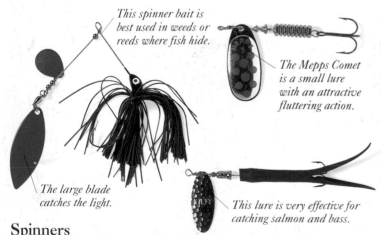

This spinner bait is best used in weeds or reeds where fish hide.

The Mepps Comet is a small lure with an attractive fluttering action.

The large blade catches the light.

This lure is very effective for catching salmon and bass.

Spinners
On a spinner, a metal blade rotates as the lure is pulled through the water. The rotation sends out vibrations and the blade catches the light, so the lure looks like a small fish. Sometimes tassels of plastic or wool are added to entice the fish further.

Down she goes!
This pike has taken a lure fished close to the surface and is now plunging toward the bottom in an attempt to escape. Keep pressure on the fish and do not let it get into any underwater snags – you do not want to leave a fish with hooks in its mouth.

A leaping bass

Many fish, like this bass, will immediately jump out of the water when they are hooked. Drop your rod tip just a little to slacken pressure on the line; otherwise, you might find that it breaks. This is a dangerous moment because the hooks can easily be thrown free.

This bass is perfectly hooked in the lip.

The Heron is a king-size lure used for catching pike.

The rippled finish of the Abu Atom catches and reflects the light as it is pulled through the water.

The Atlantic spoon is very effective when fished slowly.

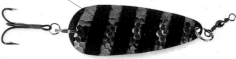

Spoons

A spoon is a lure made of shaped sheet metal. When cast and retrieved from the bank, spoons wobble through the water and attract predatory fish with their shiny finish and bright colors. Their action depends on the style of retrieve, so wind in erratically to make them look like fish in distress.

Your quarry

Lure fishing is perfect for all sorts of predators. In general, the smaller the fish, the smaller the lure you should use. For example, a Mepps Comet lure would be perfect for this perch (right), but for really big fish, like pike, you should move up in size and use the Heron or the Stingfish. Look for signs in the water to help you decide which lure to use. For instance, if prey fish are showering out of the water, you will know a hunter is at work. If there are no signs, you'll have to observe every feature in the water very carefully. Think out each cast. Change the speed of retrieve. Move your rod tip around so the lure follows different tracks through the water. In cold weather, try to fish as deep as possible – you actually feel your spinner or spoon bounce along the bottom, where the big fish are lying.

Bait fishing

I**T IS VERY IMPORTANT** to make
sure that your bait is in tip-top condition.
Wary fish will not accept old or stale bait.
Whatever you use, it should have an
appealing aroma. It should also look fresh;
a live, wriggling worm is far more attractive
than a dead one. Make sure that your bait is
on the right-size hook. It is no good having
a huge bait on a tiny hook or vice versa.
Never be afraid to go for an unusual bait.
Fish wise up quickly, so something out of
the ordinary works well to fool them.

Getting the bait down
Most fish will take bait that is lying on the bottom, so you have to
get both the hook bait and any loose bait down there quickly. Both
chumfeeders and bait droppers accomplish this task. Pack the feeder
tightly, cast it out, and it will release its load of bait on the bed.

A huge variety
There are many types of bait, and some, like these
particle baits, need boiling to soften them. These are
small and plentiful, encouraging fish to feed in a frenzy
so that they suck up the bait without inspecting it properly.

*These high-protein (HP) baits are
made of milk proteins,
eggs, soy flour, wheat germ,
animal proteins, flavorings,
and colorings.*

Cooked lima beans

Cooked Great Northen beans

Cooked pasta

Cooked chickpeas

Cooked dried peas

Peanuts

Raw vetch seeds

Cooked vetch seeds

Processed hemp

Cooked corn

Cooked rice

Baits from the kitchen
Some of the most useful baits can be found
in the kitchen cabinet or refrigerator.
However, ask permission before
disappearing with the evening meal!

Bread
Use bread that is as fresh as possible. Push
the hook through a small piece and squeeze
tightly around the shank. The rest should
remain fluffy so it expands in the water.

*Leave the end
of the sausage
crumbly so that
bits break off
and attract
the fish.*

*Make sure your fingers
are clean before baiting up.*

Sausage
There are many types of already cooked
sausages available today – just look at the
range in your local supermarket. Sausages
make excellent baits because fish can smell
their strong aroma even in cloudy water
conditions. Cut a suitable length of sausage
and thread the hook through. Make sure the
hook point projects through any tough skin.

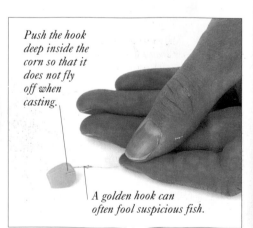

*Push the hook
deep inside the
corn so that it
does not fly
off when
casting.*

*A golden hook can
often fool suspicious fish.*

Corn
Nearly all fish adore the tiny, sweet,
yellow grains of corn. Use corn that is
as fresh and sugary as possible. You can
thread one grain onto a small hook, or
five or six grains onto a bigger hook for
large fish. Try varying the size of the
hook and the number of grains if you
are not getting any bites.

Natural baits

Some of the best baits are also the simplest, such as those that you find in and around the water. After all, this is what the fish are used to eating every day, and their suspicions are unlikely to be aroused. The other advantage is that baits that you find around you are free!

You can dig your own lugworms at low tide on the mudflats. However, make sure that the tide is on its way out.

All sorts of mussels are good for catching both freshwater and sea fish. Do not use them if the water has limited stocks.

The predator

For big, aggressive predators like pike, you cannot beat fresh fish, their natural food. Try using dead sea fish as baits; sprats, herrings, mackerel, and sardines all make excellent deadbaits for pike. Small freshwater fish also work well, especially those with silvery scales.

The river pantry

For chub, barbel, roach, dace, and a host of other river species, you can find the best foodstuffs under any big stone or rock. Probably the best bait is the caddis grub, which makes a little cocoon for itself. Ease the shell off the rock and gently pry the grub out of its cover. Two caddis grubs on a fairly small hook are perfect bait for both bobber and bottom fishing.

Other good baits include eels, all types of nymph, freshwater shrimp, and grasshoppers.

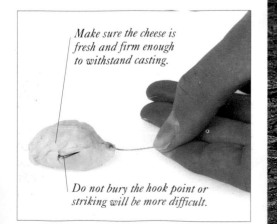

Make sure the cheese is fresh and firm enough to withstand casting.

Do not bury the hook point or striking will be more difficult.

Cheese

Cheese is another excellent bait for murky water conditions when visibility is low. Creamy cheeses are especially good if they are mixed with dry bread. Knead the two together until you get a firm paste that sticks to the hook and stays there during casting. Most species love moldy cheese, so do not be afraid of using smelly leftovers.

Bobber fishing

BOBBERS CAN BE MADE of quill, wood, cork, or plastic. You can use a bobber to fish bait at various depths, from just under the surface of the water, to right on the bottom. If you are fishing a river, you can try trotting a bait under a bobber, which involves allowing it to move with the current. Most important, a bobber gives you an immediate bite indication so that you can strike early and not deep hook your fish.

A bobber rod
The ideal bobber rod should be around 10–13 ft (3–4 m) long, light enough to allow use of comparatively light lines, and comfortable enough to hold all day. It should also have a flexible tip section.

Use brightly colored bobber tips in dark, shaded waters.

Use enough shot to pull down the bobber so that only the tip is visible.

The ideal location
A deepish channel close to an island is a perfect bobber-fishing location. Fish will funnel through areas like this as they move around the lake. Choppy, shallow water helps to hide your bobber from the eyes of wary fish.

Finding the depth
Start fishing your bait close to the surface, then move it closer and closer to the bottom until you find where the fish are feeding.

A piece of corn next to a maggot makes an appetizing bait cocktail!

In some places, maggots are used as bait. They work best when fresh and lively.

Bobber fishing
It is important to choose the right bobber for the job. On still water, a straight-bodied waggler-type bobber is perfect. Use one that is heavy enough to cast easily and is clearly visible, even at a distance in rough water.

Hold the end of the line firmly, leaving a few inches above your fingers.

Make sure the attachment eye is free of varnish so that the line passes through easily.

1 Thread the line carefully through all the rod eyes. Always put the line through the center of the eye. Leave the bail arm of the reel open so that the line comes off the spool easily. Make sure that the line does not loop off too early and get tangled.

2 When you are fishing still water, attach just the bottom end of the bobber to the line. Wind the line through the bottom eyes a couple of times so that it hangs securely in position. Alternatively, you can secure the bobber by placing shot above and below it.

When casting, look carefully at the spot on the water you want the bobber to settle in.

Hold the rod steady over your head before casting.

Before a fishing trip, check your slingshot elastic for signs of wear.

3 Hold the rod vertically over your shoulder in line with the area of water you want to cast toward. Move the rod smoothly and powerfully. Once the rod is in the two o'clock position in front of you, let the line fly out. Keep your finger close to the spool of the reel so you can stop the line when the bobber has reached the right place.

4 Scatter loose feed around your bobber with a slingshot. This is more accurate than throwing the bait by hand since it allows you to position bait at greater distances. The smell of the feed should draw the fish out into the open water. Do not overdo the bait. Start with a small amount and increase it gradually if you are getting many bites.

Reading the bites

Every fish has its own bite, giving a specific indication on the bobber. Strike too soon, and you will miss the fish; strike too late, and the bait may be swallowed. As a rule of thumb, always strike early. If you are missing bites, delay a second or so each time until you begin to hook the fish. As your experience grows, your timing will improve.

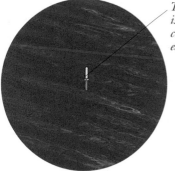

The bobber tip is brightly colored for easy visibility.

The correct setting

The bobber is just visible above the water line. It is correctly shotted so that any movement will be detected at once. The shot rests on the bottom of the pool and the bait is about 6 in (15 cm) away.

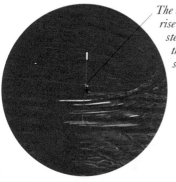

The bobber will rise slowly and steadily when the bottom shot is lifted.

Taking the bait

As a small carp or sunfish takes and sucks at the bait, the shot that has cocked the bobber is lifted. The bobber itself begins to rise in the water. Do not strike yet because the fish is still mouthing the bait.

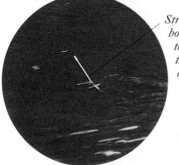

Strike before the bobber begins to dip under the surface of the water.

The right time to strike

The bobber teeters at a 45° angle to the water as the fish moves away with the bait in its mouth. Strike now, before the fish feels the weight of the shot and spits out the bait.

Bottom fishing

BOTTOM FISHING is placing a bait on the bottom of the river or lake that you are fishing, usually with a weight to hold it in place. It is particularly useful when you are hoping to ambush a big fish and you have to keep the bait in the same position for a long time. There is no bobber to indicate when you have a bite, so other forms of indication are needed to avoid ending up with a deeply hooked fish.

The ideal location
This is a perfect spot for using weights. The thick rushes at the far end of the lake are superb habitat for all types of bottom feeders, and you can sit a little bit back from the water's edge, well screened by the long grasses.

The rod
At about 9 ft (3 m) in length, weight-fishing rods tend to be shorter than bobber rods. Try to match the strength of the rod with the power and size of the fish.

Using a bobbin

A bobbin is a very easy and efficient way of determining whether you have a bite. The bobbin can either be a piece of bread, a cork, or a cylinder of aluminum foil tied to the line between the first and second rod eyes. The bobbin will move when a fish takes the bait.

Night fishing
A small glowing isotope instead of a piece of bread shines brightly on a dark night.

2 Wait until you see the bobbin moving either up or down in a positive manner, and then set the hook. It is important to time your response correctly, because if you wait too long, the fish will either drop the bait or be deeply hooked.

1 Sit comfortably with your rod on a rest and point it directly toward the bait. You will know you have attracted a fish when the bobbin starts to jump and then either rises or falls smoothly. If the bobbin drops to the ground, it means a fish has taken the bait and is coming toward you. If it rises, it means the fish is moving away from you.

Only strike when you notice a definite movement from the bobbin.

Hold the rod where the reel seat meets the handle.

Quivertipping

If you fish a river in the UK, you may find quivertips being used to indicate bites. A quivertip is a very fine piece of carbon inserted into the end of a normal rod, and it is very sensitive to any biting fish. Quivertips come in a variety of lengths and strengths, all made to match the power of the river and the weight of the lead you are using. Look for a tip painted red and/or white, which makes it very visible against the sky or background trees. A bite can be a series of either trembles or knocks on the tip, but sometimes the tip will slam around, leaving you in no doubt.

The gentle curve of this weight-fishing rod is perfect for big fish.

Line up your tip against any light background, so that it is easier to watch over a long period of time.

Keep your grip relaxed and easy.

1 Place the quivertip where you can clearly see it, such as against an area of white water. Try to get just a slight bend in the quivertip – if it is too acute, you will not be able to see the action of a biting fish.

2 Position yourself on the bank so that you are ready to spring into action the instant you see a bite indicated on the quivertip. Always try to travel light, so that if you are unsuccessful in one spot, you can move on to try another.

Watching the bite

Make sure that the bread you use for your bread indicator is as fresh as possible, so that it clings to the line. You can alter the size of the bobbin according to the wind and current. In very calm conditions, when there is little or no undertow, a small bobbin will be adequate. In rougher weather conditions, you will have to use a larger, heavier bobbin. Make sure that the bobbin hangs steadily beneath the rod.

1 Before you cast, decide where you want to fish. If you are fishing close to the bank, you can just swing the bait out into the water with an underarm movement. For longer distances, you will need an overhead cast and a heavier bobbin.

Feeling the line

Touching the line is the most sensitive way of feeling for a bite, especially on a river. It is very exciting because you actually feel the fish nosing your bait, taking the hook, and swimming away with it. This is a straightforward technique, and the only equipment you need is your fingers!

2 Once you have completed the cast, you can simply tighten up and place the bobbin on your line between the bottom two rod eyes. Keep your hand on the rod butt and watch the bobbin carefully for any signs of activity.

Hold your rod comfortably, pointing toward the bait. Then pull the line away near the reel and just slip it around your fingers, so that you can sense any tugs the second you get a bite.

Surf fishing

CASTING FROM THE SHORE into surf is one of the most physical forms of fishing. Correct technique rather than brute force is the key; otherwise, you will spoil your body action. Study the basic movements shown below and build up a good, smooth rhythm. You will find that your casting distances will gradually increase with practice.

The ideal location

Surf fishing is not always about casting long distances. Where there are rocks and cliffs, you will find that many fish species such as bass and flounder will come in very close.

Safety near water
Always watch out for an incoming tide. Never risk being cut off by the rising water.

Try to get your left hand as close to shoulder level as you can.

Look upward to follow the direction of the cast.

Extend your right arm.

Pull the rod across your body.

Bend your right leg.

Adopt a comfortable stance.

Move your weight from the right leg to the left leg.

Casting

This type of casting is known as surf casting, and it is really suitable for only fairly clean, flat beaches. Always remember that the rod should follow you rather than be pushed ahead of you in an uncomfortable way. Get used to moving your head into the casting direction and untwisting your body smoothly. This should all become one fluid movement once you have practiced it enough.

1 Set the reel for casting, with your weight and hook hanging just over 3 ft (1 m) from the tip ring. Put your thumb over the line. Twist your body to the left, putting your weight on your right leg.

2 Turn your head to face the cast direction and untwist your body. Start to straighten your left arm. Your right hand should move in close to your chest.

3 Transfer your body weight to your left leg. This increases the casting speed and makes for a really long cast. Move your right hand up toward eye level.

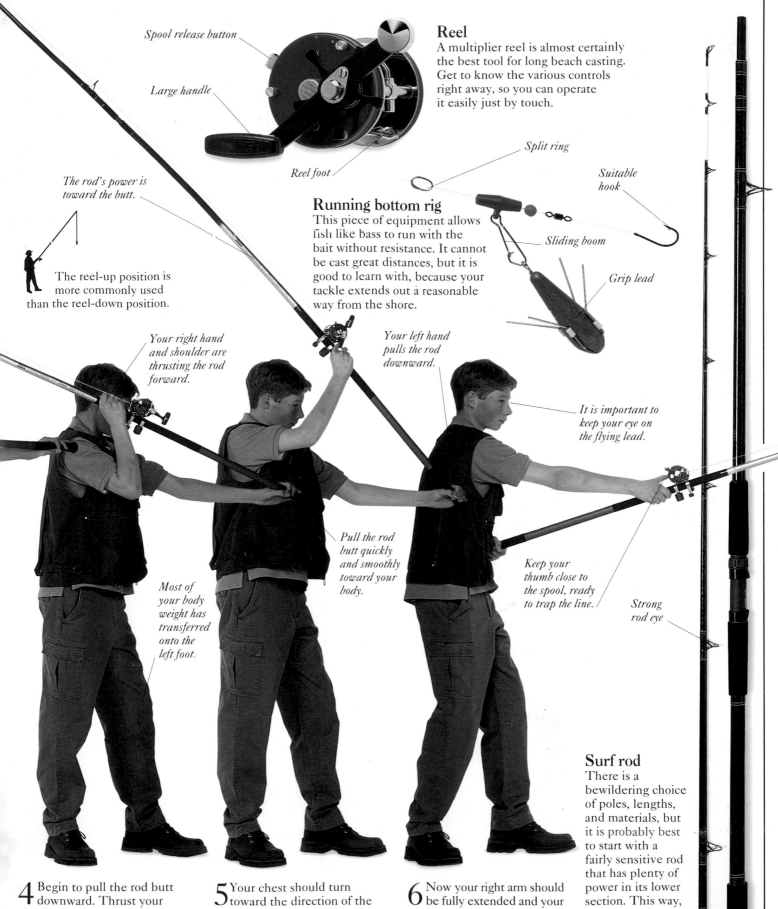

Spool release button

Large handle

Reel foot

Reel
A multiplier reel is almost certainly the best tool for long beach casting. Get to know the various controls right away, so you can operate it easily just by touch.

Split ring

Suitable hook

Running bottom rig
This piece of equipment allows fish like bass to run with the bait without resistance. It cannot be cast great distances, but it is good to learn with, because your tackle extends out a reasonable way from the shore.

Sliding boom

Grip lead

The rod's power is toward the butt.

The reel-up position is more commonly used than the reel-down position.

Your right hand and shoulder are thrusting the rod forward.

Your left hand pulls the rod downward.

It is important to keep your eye on the flying lead.

Most of your body weight has transferred onto the left foot.

Pull the rod butt quickly and smoothly toward your body.

Keep your thumb close to the spool, ready to trap the line.

Strong rod eye

Surf rod
There is a bewildering choice of poles, lengths, and materials, but it is probably best to start with a fairly sensitive rod that has plenty of power in its lower section. This way, you should be able to cast a good distance and still feel a hooked fish.

4 Begin to pull the rod butt downward. Thrust your right hand upward at the same time. Try to make this casting action one smooth continuous movement.

5 Your chest should turn toward the direction of the cast, and your rod tip should move quickly over your head. Release the line while extending your right arm.

6 Now your right arm should be fully extended and your left hand tucked in against your ribs. As soon as the lead hits the water, place your thumb over the spool again.

Reading the shoreline

AT FIRST SIGHT, the shore seems very long and the sea seems very large! Where do you begin looking for a particular species of sea fish? All sea fish have their own characteristic likes and dislikes, which makes the task of pinpointing them much easier. It is important to bear in mind seasons, depths, strength of the currents, the nature of the seabed, and the availability of cover when you are deciding where to fish and for what.

Mackerel

There are many types of mackerel, but all of them are long and streamlined, and have a markedly forked tail. Mackerel tend to move close inshore during the summer months and can be found in huge schools. It is best to drift in a boat when looking for them. Try feathers on a hook or small spinners as bait.

The mullet is often called "the gray ghost" because of its ability to slide by unnoticed.

Gray mullet

Mullet tend to move northward in the summer as the waters warm up. They feed on small organisms but will eat larger food items when they are available. You will often find mullet around harbors, which they visit during high water. There they will scavenge for all types of tidbits thrown in by passersby. Try fishing for them with light bobber tackle and a piece of bread on a small hook.

Conger eel

These big eels tend to feed by night and rest by day close to piers, breakwaters, or anywhere they can find rocks or fallen debris to give them some shelter. They can also be found close to harbors, where they feed on unwanted scraps thrown away by fishermen. To catch them you will need a wire leader, a strong rod, and hefty line. Use large fish baits anchored on the sea bottom.

All members of the wrasse family have short, stumpy bodies.

Twine spot wrasse

Wrasse are lovers of rocks and cliffs, and this is where you should try to find them. Wrasse have very strong lips and teeth, which they use to crush shellfish, abundant in these types of places. You can sometimes catch wrasse by using a bobber, but more often by putting bait on the sea bottom. For bait, use worms, crabs, and shellfish. Check the tides so that you are never cut off by rising water.

The bass has a big mouth that can open wide to eat small fish.

You will never forget the fighting spirit of a decent-size sea trout hooked in a running surf!

Sea bass

Sea bass move close inshore during the summer months, and you will often find them foraging up river mouths and feeding in brackish water. Look for them around rocks and off piers – you may also find them where the surf breaks over sand. You can catch bass using worms and crabs, but possibly the most exciting way to pursue them is with plugs and spinners. This method keeps you mobile, searching new areas until you find fish.

Sea trout

Sea trout are generally caught in rivers, but they can also be taken from the shore. Look for sea trout around rocks and river mouths or where there is a good surf running. Sea trout are great foragers, and you can catch them on worms, crabs, or small fish baits. The most fun of all, however, is to spin for sea trout with silver-colored spoons or plugs about 4–5 in (10–12 cm) in length.

Most flatfish lie along sandy seabeds, feeding on worms, small crabs, and a variety of other marine foodstuffs.

Flatfish

Flatfish range from the smaller flounder and sole, right up to the huge halibut. They tend to be most active at night, but you can catch them during the day if you fish the bait on the sea bottom. Try minnows, strips of squid, or a bunch of worms. Flatfish sometimes attack small spinners cast a long way out from the shore.

Playing and landing your fish

PLAYING A FISH of any real size calls for patience, a cool head, and a lot of thought. Do not panic when you have finally gotten that long-awaited fish on the end of your line. Practice the skills shown here, get to know your reel controls and how to maximize the power of your rod, and with any luck, that fish will be yours.

Playing the fish

It is a good idea to practice at home on dry land, with a friend being the fish and pulling the line for you. This will teach you the limits of your tackle so that you know when you have to give line and when you can wind it in. This can save disappointment later on the riverbank.

Notice how this rod bends along its length to take the strain of a plunging fish.

1 It is important to be comfortable when you are playing a fish because some fights can be very long. Tuck the butt of the rod under your arm to give you better control and more power when lifting the rod.

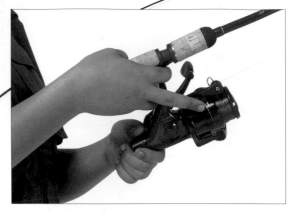

The drag

The drag mechanism, located on the back of the reel, allows the spool to rotate under pressure so that line is given to a running fish. Adjust the drag until you have exactly the right tension.

Make sure your footing is secure and your body is perfectly balanced.

When you are playing a big fish, you will find that the power of the rod is in the lower sections.

Always hold the handle of the rod firmly but comfortably.

Get used to the feel of fly line. Avoid holding it too tightly, or the monofilament leader will break.

Using fly tackle

Playing a fish on fly tackle is particularly thrilling. The fly rod is usually very light, so you can feel every plunge that the fish makes. When a hooked fish jumps, remember to lower your rod tip a fraction to give the line a little slack.

1 You may not have to use the reel very much when you are playing a fish on fly tackle. Instead, use your hands, letting line out when the fish runs and then retrieving the line when you sense that the fish is tiring.

Keep the rod up
It is important to remember to keep the rod as high as possible to cushion all the plunges of the fish.

2 When the fish takes the fly and sets off in haste, feed line out to it through your fingers. When all the loose line around your feet is taken up by the running fish, it will begin to strip line off your reel in the normal fashion. You will soon sense how much pressure to exert on the fly line so that it feeds smoothly to the fish without breaking.

Keep the rod up high as the fish comes in to the bank.

2 The critical moment is when the fish is getting close. Do not rush it to the net. Watch carefully, and once the fish is motionless and on its side, draw it over the submerged landing net. Then lift the net, and the fish will fall into the meshes.

Hold the handle of the net firmly and with control.

Always choose a net that is large enough to engulf the catch.

Catching and landing the fish

On the riverbank, in the excitement of having hooked a fish, it is tempting to forget all you have learned and try to heave the fish over your shoulder and onto land. Avoid this at all costs! Instead, remember the rules, keep a steady pressure on the fish, and, if your tackle is secure, you should be successful. Check your line and knots before casting because the fish will expose any weakness. Also, make sure your landing net is close at hand. You do not want to waste time looking for it when a fish is tired and ready to land.

1 Once the bobber has gone under, you are ready to strike. Put in just the right amount of pressure to set the hook, but not so much that the line breaks. You will have to strike quite hard for long distances, but for striking close by, a simple flick of the wrist will do.

2 Once again, keep the rod high. You will find that this gives a cushioning effect, absorbing any dashes the fish might make and protecting the line as well.

Notice that the landing net is close at hand, ready for action.

Set the drag on your fly reel so that it gives line to a running fish under pressure.

3 Once the fish surfaces and you can pull its head out of the water, you will know it is beaten and ready for the net. Do not try to net a fish if it is still very lively. If the fish is heavy, be prepared to lift the net by the frame rather than the handle.

A beaten fish, too tired to struggle any further

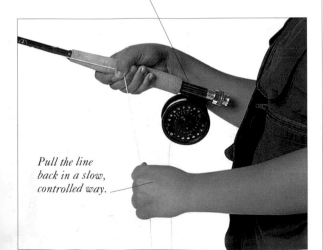

Pull the line back in a slow, controlled way.

3 When the fish at last grows tired, start maneuvering it back toward the bank. Trap the line against the rod handle with the fingers of one hand. With your free hand, slowly pull the line back in, avoiding any jerky movements. Try to anticipate the fish's movements and be prepared to give it line if it wants to run out again.

4 Keep the net fairly still in the water and draw the fish over it. Once you are quite sure that that the entire fish is over the rim, lift the net gently and steadily out of the water and onto the bank. Do not pursue the fish with the net, or you run the risk of knocking it off the hook.

Releasing your catch

WELL DONE! You have caught your fish, and it is lying there in the net. However, remember that you have a great responsibility to treat that fish as carefully and considerately as you can, and to return it to the water unharmed. In the water, fish may look strong and powerful, but bear in mind that the effect on them of being lifted out of their natural environment can be very traumatic.

 Safety near water
Be extra careful when standing on slippery banks.

Notice the way I am holding this fish, with my hands away from any vital organs.

A prize catch
I was very proud of this catch and wanted a photograph. However, it was a hot day, and I knew that this would cause the fish some distress, so the shot had to be taken very quickly. I had already focused the camera before I took the fish from the water, and I made sure I held it over the water's edge in case it wriggled free.

Unhooking and releasing

Always treat any fish you catch as gently as you can, whatever its size. Make sure that you wet your hands before you handle the fish, or you may disturb the coat of slime or mucus that surrounds the fish and protects it from disease.

As you become used to handling fish, you will know just how much pressure to exert.

1 Once you have lifted your fish out of the water, it is important that you hold it firmly to prevent it from wriggling free and falling to the ground. Remember not to squeeze it too hard though, or you could damage its vital organs.

2 If you are right handed, hold the fish in your left hand and take the hook out with your stronger fingers. If the hook is barbless, it should slip free very easily. Should there be a problem, simply wriggle the hook gently with your fingers and it will soon drop away.

Under pressure
Always keep cool when you are handling a fish and try not to panic – even when it starts to wriggle!

3 This is a critical moment. You have to return the fish to the water, but you must also be aware of your own safety. If the bank is high, look for a safe entry point nearby. When you place the fish in the water, make sure you crouch down on the bank in a comfortable, stable position. If possible, have a friend there in case you fall. Never take chances.

4 Watch your fish very carefully after you have slipped it into the water. Do not release it until it is strong enough to hold its own against the current. Never let a fish go off downriver belly-up, because it will be unable to right itself and will certainly die. If you can, let the fish lie in the soft weeds along the bank until it recovers.

Releasing underwater

If you are fishing a stretch of shallow river where you can wade safely, it is often possible to release a fish completely underwater. This reduces any stress the fish may suffer. Unless a fish is particularly unusual, you do not really have to look at it carefully. The bite and the fight should be exciting enough, and then you can wish it a fond farewell! Never use a keep-net, unless you are fishing in a competition, since it causes the fish physical and mental harm.

1 This chub is now exhausted and ready for landing, but it is not really necessary to remove it from the water to be admired and then released. Bringing it onto the bank will cause a certain amount of stress, which can be avoided by unhooking it entirely underwater.

The fish is on its side and is tired enough for the hook to be removed.

2 With a fairly small fish like this one, there is no need even to use a landing net. Lower your rod to take the tension off the line and slip the hook out with your fingers. If the hook is barbless, it will slip free at once. Get ready to support the fish with your free hand.

3 The fish is now ready for release, even though it has not yet broken the surface. To give it some time to recover its strength before it swims away into the powerful current, hold it facing upstream until you feel its fins begin to pulse and its muscles flex. There is now no danger of it rolling over and being unable to right itself, so you can let it go.

Fish directory

THERE ARE NEARLY 20,000 types of fish swimming in the world's freshwaters and seas, and it is exciting to get to know as much as possible about the many different species and their various characteristics. Even though it would be impossible to catch them all, it is good to look for as many different types as you can, rather than to specialize in one species. In doing so, you will learn much about the amazing world that exists beneath the water's surface.

The pike's fins are heavily camouflaged.

The dark spot on the dorsal fin is a hallmark of the bluegill.

Bluegill

The bluegill is the most popular panfish in North America, and it is distributed throughout most of the US. It is a good fighter, although it rarely grows very large. It can be caught on flies, small spinners, and different types of bait. Look for it sheltering in weeds or among tree roots.

Large fins give the bluegill plenty of power.

The fully formed tail fin suggests a fish born in the wild.

The huge tail fin gives the carp its power.

The long, muscular body of the sturgeon makes it a great fighter.

Carp

The carp is the most popular freshwater fish in Europe. It grows to at least 60 lbs (27 kg), fights very hard, and is difficult to outwit. You can catch carp either on the bottom or with baits floating on the surface.

Sturgeon

There are around 20 types of sturgeon swimming the waters of the world, and many of them can be caught when fishing. These fish can easily grow to 300 lbs (140 kg) or more and are generally caught using a large fish bait close to the bottom. Sea tackle will usually be needed to land fish like this.

The sturgeon uses its pointed nose for digging up prey from the silt.

The position of the eyes allows the pike to see prey fish swimming overhead.

The mottled flanks of the pike allow it to blend in with its background.

Big pectorals give the pike swift acceleration.

Pike
Pike are the supreme freshwater predators of the northern hemisphere and are popular sport fish. A 20-lb (9-kg) pike is a good size, but they can grow to 40 lbs (18 kg) or more. Pike are at home in both rivers and still water and are usually found lurking among reeds, sunken logs, and boulders.

Salmon
There cannot be a more dramatic and amazing fish than the salmon. Watch them leap waterfalls and overcome all obstacles in their journey from the sea back into freshwater to spawn and die.

Chub have big, brassy scales and a thick, heavy body.

Chub
The chub is a medium-size European freshwater fish great for fishing, because it will take almost any type of bait in any water conditions.

The trout's large mouth allows it to eat fish as well as insects.

Brown trout
The brown trout varies greatly in size and appearance. There are more than 50 types of this species in Europe alone. It is a very popular sport fish, since it has a suspicious nature and is very hard to catch.

The spiny dorsal fin is partly joined to the soft-rayed second dorsal.

Large-mouth bass
The large-mouth bass is arguably the favorite sport fish in North America. It has been widely distributed around the world because of its power, cunning, and willingness to attack lures, flies, and baits.

The bass has a deep, mottled-green body and a pronounced lateral line.

The eye of the zander is opaque, giving it a glassy look.

Zander
The European zander is very much like its North American cousin, the walleye. Both species grow to 15–20 lbs (7–9 kg) and feed especially well at dusk, through the night, and at dawn. Try using small, dead fish or medium-size spoons and plugs to catch them.

41

Taking it further

ONE OF THE WONDERFUL things about fishing is that it can lead you to exotic, faraway places. As your experience increases, your confidence will grow and you will want to take on new challenges, catch new types of fish, and learn new skills. No matter how many years you spend fishing, there will always be more exciting new waters to discover.

Wild river fishing

The really big, gushing rivers of the world present challenging opportunities for both fly and lure fishing. You have to learn to control your tackle in the swiftest of waters, where huge fish often lurk. It is hair-raising, white-knuckle stuff that demands both your technique and your tackle to be flawless!

Fly tying

On long, dark winter evenings, you may want to try tying your own flies. Making perfect imitations of the natural flies on which fish feed is an exact, truly satisfying science. You may find that your own flies are more successful than expensive, store-bought ones.

The mighty mahseer

This fisherman looks delighted with his catch – and no wonder! This enormous mahseer was caught in a huge river in southern India and fought for more than an hour and a half in fast-flowing water. It weighed more than 90 lbs (40 kg) and was a record for that stretch of water. Truly the catch of a lifetime!

More than 100 years ago, British officers in India used the mahseer's huge scales as playing cards.

Boat fishing

As you become more experienced, you may want to move away from the bank and try the different skills involved in boat fishing. Boat control is a whole new art in itself and requires much practice. Landing a large fish from a boat can be very tricky, since it demands perfect timing.

Never do anything quickly when you are in a boat. Every movement should be calm and controlled. It is advisable to wear a lifejacket.

Fishing the wilderness

Here I am fishing for colossal catfish on a wilderness river in the Himalayas of Nepal. It took three days to reach this remote water, where, I was told, no other European had fished before. This was the perfect location: deep water, a gliding current, and numerous rocks for huge prey fish to hide behind.

The tropical seas

You may be lucky enough to travel to exotic places such as Christmas Tree Island, above, and fish the warm oceans that surround it. The shallows in tropical seas tend to be richer in fish than those in cooler waters. Countless varieties of fish roam the shallows (called the Flats) of this crystal-clear water. This snapper has come in close to the shore to feed off the colorful coral reefs.

Night fishing

Nothing can beat the serenity of night fishing for utter peace. It is often a good idea to fish at night if waters are so clear that you are visible to the fish in the daytime.

Considerate fishing

R EMEMBER THAT WHENEVER you are fishing you are a representative of our sport. Always read the rules that the club or owner has laid down for the water; they are for everybody's good, yours included, and you should follow them to the letter. Avoid putting any life at risk, whether it is yours, another fishing enthusiast's, or that of a fish, a bird, livestock, or a wild animal. Enjoy the beauty of the river, but always remember to be considerate!

Kayakers and canoeists

Remember that we are not the only people with a right to use the water. Swimmers, walkers, sailors, water-skiers, and even scuba divers all enjoy water sports. Paddlers can seem a problem on some rivers, but they will nearly always move across river and out of your way. Be reassured that most fish are not disturbed by the presence of light boats like these.

Kingfisher

Sit quietly on the riverbank and you will hear the thin piping call of the kingfisher as it speeds past in a blur of blue. If you are lucky, this fellow fish-lover may actually land on your rod tip. It is a rare and magical moment that should be treasured.

Dusk and dawn are the best times to see an otter.

Otter

Otters are quite large and very shy, so do not confuse them with the bolder, smaller mink that frequent so many riverbanks. The otter is a sure sign that the water you are fishing is well stocked, so it is a welcome sight. If you do see an otter, congratulate yourself; it is proof that you are quiet, considerate, and respectful of the countryside and its wildlife.

Closing gates

Always shut gates behind you; otherwise, livestock could escape onto roads, causing fatal accidents. Be sure that you shut a gate properly. Check that you have fastened it exactly as you found it, since it could come loose in a strong wind or if horses push against it.

Countryside awareness

Always stay on well-defined pathways, especially if you are walking to the fishing area through crops. Try to avoid climbing over and perhaps damaging fences wherever possible. If you are fishing with a dog, keep your dog on a leash. Never light a fire in windy, dry conditions.

Cross bridges carefully if they are slippery after rain.

Picking up your line

Never leave discarded line on the bank, for it can easily become entangled in the legs of animals and birds. Unable to fly or run off, they are doomed to a lingering death. Take special care never to leave a baited hook on any piece of line, in case a bird decides to eat it and dies as a result.

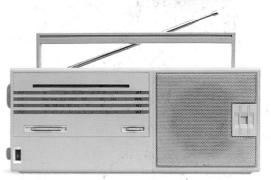

Discarded line will take years to rot.

Noise

Noise travels very freely over water. You can be heard by other people fishing who may seem a long way off. Please do not shout or run around, and most important, do not have a radio blaring. Nearly all people go fishing to escape the hustle and bustle of modern-day life, not to be reminded of it.

Show consideration for all enclosed animals.

Take notice of the signs

Waterside signs are put up for your good or the good of the water. If you are asked to take only four fish, that is because any more would ruin the chances of other fishing enthusiasts. Watch out for any danger signs. They might warn about deep water, slippery banks, or overhead power lines.

FOUR FISH LIMIT

Always read signs.

Glossary

You will find many of these words useful during your days on the river.

A

Adipose fin The small, fleshy fin on the back of fish from the salmon family.

Avon bobber A bobber used for fishing in fast water. The top of the bobber is fairly buoyant, which allows it to ride the current well.

B

Backing Fine, strong braid or nylon of 320 ft (100 m) or more put on a fly reel underneath the standard fly line. Essential for playing large fish.

Backwind Giving line to a running fish by simply letting go of the handle and letting the reel move in reverse. Not used very often today, since drags are more efficient.

Bag limit The limit trout fisheries put on the amount of fish that can be caught.

Bail arm The metal arm on an open-faced reel. It helps to guide the line onto the spool.

Barb A sharp piece of metal on the hook.

Barbles Whiskery fingers of flesh that hang down from the sides of many fishes' mouths.

Bite A term for when a fish has taken the bait.

Bivvies A common name for bivouacs.

Boiled bait This is usually made out of eggs, flavorings, colorings, soy, and other additives, boiled and rolled into small balls for easy casting.

Bottom fishing The style of fishing that puts a bait right on the bottom, often anchored by a heavy load.

Braid lines A thinner alternative to nylon lines.

Breaking strain The weight limit that lines can carry before they break, for example, 2.2 lbs (1 kg).

Butt The rod handle.

C

Carbon fiber Very light and strong material, used in most fishing rods.

Casters The chrysalis form of maggots. The bluebottle develops within the shell and emerges when ready to fly.

Chumfeeders Cylinders of plastic or metal, attached to a line close to the hook, that take samples of bait down to the bed of a river or lake.

Cocked The position of a bobber when it is sitting vertically in the water.

D

Dorsal fin The fin at the top of a fish's back. These take many forms; in the perch and bass family they are spiked.

Down-rigger A mechanism that takes spinning baits down into the deep areas of large lakes.

Drag A mechanism in the reel that allows line to be taken off under different pressures.

Dry-fly fishing Fishing a floating fly on the surface of the water.

E

Eddy A piece of slow and often deep water, just off the main current of a river.

Eyes The rings on a rod which guide the line.

F

False casting Moving a rod backward and forward a few times before casting. This is done in fly-fishing to work more line out before letting it lie on the surface of the water.

Floating line Used when fishing a dry fly or a small nymph just under the surface.

Forceps Scissorlike tool used to remove hooks from a fish's mouth.

Foul-hooked Any fish that is not hooked on the mouth.

Fry Tiny fish that have just emerged from eggs after spawning time.

G

Game fish Fish belonging to the salmon family (including trout and grayling).

Groundbait Any bait thrown into a fishing area to stimulate fish to feed.

H

Hatch A group of newly hatched flies that stimulate trout and grayling into feeding.

I

Ice fishing Fishing through ice.

J

Jerk baits Very big plugs that are fished with stiff, short rods. They are pulled or jerked though the water erratically.

Jigging Fishing from boats with baits directly beneath the rods, moving the rod up and down to give it life. Often a small spinner or a little plastic worm is used as bait.

L

Landing net A net used to scoop a beaten fish out of the water and to lay it onto the bank.

Leader A stretch of nylon that is attached to the end of a fly line. The imitation fly is tied to the point of the leader.

Leads Lead weights used to sink a bait. Leads weighing 1/2–4 oz (14–110 gm) are used in freshwater bottom fishing. In sea fishing the leads can be much heavier.

Lie A place where a fish, generally a trout, likes to live. A trout will have its own lie for most of its life.

Live bait Any bait that is live, such as fish, frogs, or grasshoppers.

Loose feed Samples of the hook bait scattered around a fishing area to encourage fish to feed.

Lures A general name given to spinners, spoons, and plugs – all imitations of small fish.

M

Mending the line Correcting a line that has been pushed into a bow shape by a river's current. It is done by lifting the rod tip, allowing the bobber to travel downstream in a natural way.

Monofilament Nylon line that is difficult to see in the water. Necessary for freshwater fishing.

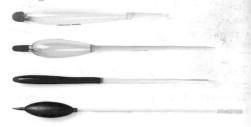

Mucus The protective slimy coating on most fish that prevents disease.

N

Nymph fishing Using small flies that imitate nymphs in water to catch trout and grayling.

P

Panfish Small American freshwater fish, such as bluegill or sunfish.

Plastic worms Imitation worms that are attached onto a weighted hook and usually jigged for small predators like perch zander.

Playing a fish Line, reel, and rod control when winding in a bite.

Polaroid glasses Glasses with special lenses that filter out the reflections on the water's surface. They make it possible to see what the fish are doing under the water.

Poles Very long, light fishing rods – often up to 50 ft (15 m) in length. These are used in match fishing to catch lots of small fish quickly.

Pool A slow, deep area of water found along a river, often behind rocks or fallen trees.

Prey fish Fish that are the diet of predators.

R

Reel seat A device that attaches a reel to a rod.

Riffle A fast, shallow, broken area of river where you will find trout and grayling.

Rise The action of a fish coming to the surface and sipping in a floating insect.

Rod rest A metal stick with a V-shaped top designed to cradle the rod when it is not being held. Very useful for bottom fishing.

Run When a fish darts away from the person fishing once it has been hooked.

S

Scales Hard pieces of bony tissue that protect a fish's body. The age of a fish can be read from the growth ring on an individual scale.

Seasons Nearly all fish have seasons when they can be caught and when they must be left alone. Fish are generally considered out of season during their spawning period.

Shot Weights that are used to present the bait at different depths.

Sinking line A line used in fly-fishing so that flies reach trout and salmon near the bottom of a river or lake.

Snag An underwater obstruction.

Sonar An electronic device attached to a boat, which gives a reading of how deep the water is. Sometimes it will show up schools of fish or large individual fish.

Spool The part of the reel that holds the line.

Stalking A method of fishing by observing the fish in the water. It requires great care and skill.

Strike The moment when a fish grabs the bait.

Swim The area of water being fished, especially with bait.

T

Take A fish biting upon a fly (especially grayling or trout).

Telescopic rods Rods that can slide down into short, compact lengths.

Terminal tackle All the tackle attached to the end of the main line, such as hooks, bobbers, weights, and lures.

Test curve The strength of a rod defined by the weight needed to bend it. A typical freshwater rod has a test curve of 1 lb (0.5 kg).

Treble hook A hook with three points, usually found on all types of lures.

Trolling A method by which natural or artificial bait is pulled long distances through water behind a boat. The bait can be fished at almost any depth and is intended to resemble a live fish.

W

Wading Walking out into a river to fish an area more effectively or to get closer to the fish.

Wet fly A fly that is fished underneath the surface for trout and salmon.

Whippings The rod eyes are attached to the rod by whippings, generally made of silk.

Useful addresses

US Fish and Wildlife Service
4401 North Fairfax Drive
Arlington, VA 22203
703/358-1744
Web site: http://www.fws.gov
The USFWS conserves, protects, and enhances fish and wildlife and their habitats for the continuing benefit of the American people.

The Reel Kids Fishing Club
c/o Trevor Ruble
1100 George Edward Via
Christiansburg, VA 24073
e-mail: reelman@bev.net
This fishing education organization for children publishes the quarterly magazine Hooked for Life *and provides information on special fishing events nationwide.*

North American Fishing Club
c/o Steven F. Burke, Pres.
12301 Whitewater Drive
Suite 260
Minnetonka, MN 55343
800/843-6232
NAFC is a 500,000-member organization devoted to freshwater fishing. Its members receive North American Fisherman *seven times a year and may do product testing. Parent-child memberships are available.*

Index

Acknowledgments

Dorling Kindersley would like to thank the following people for their help in the production of this book:

Special thanks to all the young fishing enthusiasts for their patience during the photo shoots, and also their families; Ken Aske for assisting in our search for these young people; Mike Taylor and Wendy Vane-Percy for food and accommodation; Gary Barclay at Drennan International, Harris Angling, Sportfish, and Farlow's, for supplying fishing equipment; John Partridge Limited for their involvement in the project and advice; Andy Komorowski for photographic assistance; Joanna Buck, Lee Simmons, and Selina Wood for editorial assistance; and Piers Tilbury for the jacket design.

Picture credits
The publisher would like to thank the following for their kind permission to reproduce their photographs:
a = above; c = center; b = below/bottom; l = left; r = right; t = top.
Ancient Art & Architecture Collection: 5clb; **John Bailey:** 4crb, cra, cl, tl; 5b; 38tr; 42cr, b, 42–43tc; 43bcl; 44bl, c, 44–45tc;
Andrew Besley Photolibrary: 34–35c;

Biofotos: 34bl; **Richard T. Bryant:** 9cl, 40c, 40–41b; **Kevin Cullimore:** 20c, 21tr, 26tr; **Mary Evans Picture Library:** 5cr; **E.T. Archive:** 5tl; **Robert Harding Picture Library:** Michel le Coz 32tr; **Johnny Jensen:** 42b; **JPH Foto:** 9crb, 24cl, br, 25br, tl, 27tr, 35tr; **NHPA: Agence Nature** 42cl; **OSF:** Richard Davies jacket, p6–7; **Oxford Scientific Films:** E.R. Derringer 9cra; Andreas Hartl Okapia 9tr; Colin Milkins 9br; Peter Parks 7ca; **Planet Earth Pictures:** Paulo de Oliveira 35tl; Linda Pitkin 34tt; John F. Seagrim 34cl; James D. Watt 43tr.